Touchdown at Space Camp

by Judy Veramendi
illustrated by Tom Barrett

Scott Foresman

Editorial Offices: Glenview, Illinois • New York, New York
Sales Offices: Reading, Massachusetts • Duluth, Georgia
Glenview, Illinois • Carrollton, Texas • Menlo Park, California

Did you ever think about being an astronaut some day?

You don't have to wait for years and years. You can try a trip on the space shuttle right now, at Space Camp!

The first Space Camp began in 1982. The man who started this camp got his idea from a rocket scientist.

This scientist felt that children might like a camp where they are trained just like astronauts.

The scientist was right! More than 25,000 children have gone to Space Camp since the opening of the first camp in 1982.

Camps in Florida and in other countries followed that first Space Camp. Children of all ages from all over the world have enjoyed their stay at Space Camp.

Children spend one week at
Space Camp. It is a week filled with
learning and fun!

In one week all the campers get
to know what it's really like to
be an astronaut—without ever
leaving Earth!

When the campers first get to
camp, they meet other young
kids from all over the country. At
check-in, the campers find out where
and with whom they will live for the
next week. Then the roommates
double up to form bunkmates. The
rooms are called bays and have
names like Earth and Mars.

One of the first places the campers
visit is Rocket Park. Here they get to
see real rockets.

After seeing the real rockets, the campers try making their own little rockets. They will use crickets as astronauts. They work long and hard to make good rockets for their bugs. The campers don't want their "astronauts" to have a rough flight!

On another day, the campers get in a chair that tosses them five different ways. This chair gives them an idea of what it is like to be floating in space.

Campers try moving underwater. Did you ever try walking in a pool or lake? Do you remember how it felt?

Moving underwater is very much like floating in space.

Have you ever thought about living on the moon? These campers have!

They spend a day setting up their own moon base. Each camper is dressed in a spacesuit. The campers learn that they must work together to get their jobs done.

After spending a tough day on the "moon," they are happy to go back to their bays!

Finally it's the time the campers have been waiting for. They will take a trip on the shuttle!

They have worked hard all week. They are ready!

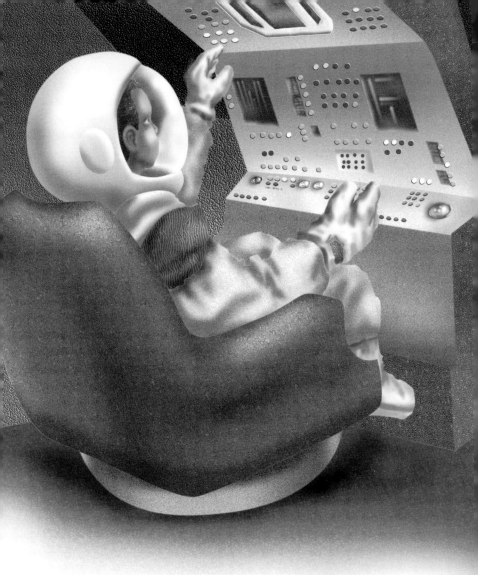

Six campers form the land crew and watch over the flight. Another six campers form the flight crew. They will take the trip into space!

The campers are happy doing the jobs they are asked to do. They know that each job is very important.

After a week of working together,
the campers get ready to go home.
Many campers stay in touch with the
friends they make at Space Camp.

Space Camp teaches kids about
space. But it also teaches kids to work
together and always try their best!